South Dartmoor pub walks

Robert Hesketh

Bossiney Books • Launceston

Other Bossiney walks books

Really short walks North Dartmoor
Shortish walks in north Cornwall
Shortish walks in north Devon
Shortish walks on Dartmoor
Shortish walks on Exmoor

First published 2005 by
Bossiney Books Ltd, Langore, Launceston, Cornwall PL15 8LD
www.bossineybooks.com

ISBN 0-1-899383-72-7

Acknowledgements
The maps are by Nick Hawken
Cover design by Heards Design Partnership
Photographs by the author except pages 5, 11, 20 and 23
which are from the publishers' own collection
Printed in Great Britain by R Booth Ltd, Mabe, Cornwall

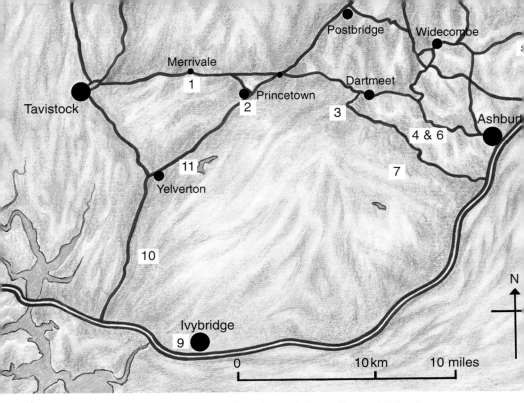

The approximate starting locations of the walks in this book

Introduction

Dartmoor is southern England's highest, largest wilderness, a walker's paradise. There is nowhere quite like it. Each rocky tor has its own unique profile whilst the marks of human activity from earlier times are everywhere – though dwarfed by the heathery wastes and steeply wooded valleys.

No area of England is richer in prehistoric remains: stone rows and circles, pounds, field boundaries, house foundations and hilltop burial chambers. Stone crosses mark ancient routes, still accessible by way of clapper bridges. Early industry brought tin streamers and miners, who cut leats to drive their simple machinery. Tramways, railways and reservoirs came later, but all meld into a wonderful landscape, much of which can only be discovered on foot.

Pubs are one of the blessings of human habitation and the natural complement to a day outdoors. Dartmoor has some of the best. Each walk features a pub, and I've generally found space for a few notes on its history and special features. Please bear in mind that the more remote pubs are family-run businesses and may close one or two days a week, especially outside the high season. Check first!

At 13km (8 1/4 miles) or less, and averaging 10.7km (6 3/4 miles), all the routes in this book can be walked in a day, some in a morning or afternoon, though it is best to start with the shorter walks if you are out of practice. The time you need depends on how fast you walk and how interested you are in what you see – you might want to spend time watching a buzzard hunting, or exploring a historic church.

Safety (please take seriously)

Walking Dartmoor is safe and trouble free – if you are prepared. In the first place the weather can change suddenly. Wind, fog or rain can appear as though out of nowhere: the rain can be intense and the temperature may drop abruptly.

Please do not go without walking boots and suitable clothing. Drinking water, map and compass, plus waterproofs and an extra layer are essential, as well as a comfortable rucksack. Many, including me, add a walking stick, mobile phone (though reception can be restricted to high points) and food to the list.

The sketch maps in this book are just that – sketches. You should go equipped with the Ordnance Survey 'Explorer OL28'.

Ticks are a potential nuisance, especially in hot, humid weather. Wearing long trousers and socks offers some protection against these tiny parasites, which can carry a viral infection, Lyme disease. If one does attach itself to you, remove it promptly and carefully with tweezers, being careful to leave none of it in your skin to minimise the risk of infection. Lock your car and don't leave valuables in it.

Access

Unenclosed moorland areas are generally open. Please keep to paths over enclosed moorland, leave gates as appropriate and keep dogs under control.

More information about Dartmoor

There is too little space in this book to explain fully what you are seeing. The following books will be helpful if you are new to the moor, each describing one of the three main phases of its human habitation:

Ancient Dartmoor, Paul White
Medieval Dartmoor, Paul White
The making of modern Dartmoor, Helen Harris

I am sure you will enjoy these walks as I have.

Robert Hesketh

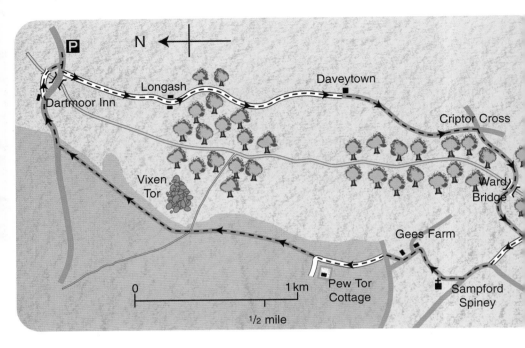

Walk 1 Merrivale and Sampford Spiney

Distance: 9.25 km (5³/4 miles) Duration of walk: 2³/4 hours
Character: A fairly gentle Dartmoor walk by footpaths and quiet lanes,
with views of several tors and the delightful church of Sampford Spiney.

Park on the B3357 Tavistock-Princetown road in a small car park
500 m east of the Dartmoor Inn at Merrivale. Turn left and walk 250 m
downhill. Turn left in front of the cottages and walk through the metal
gate signed PLEASE KEEP TO TRACK. Walk on towards Longash. After
passing a PUBLIC BRIDLEPATH sign, walk through the Longash yard,
then walk ahead, keeping the stone wall on your right.

Continue through a small oak wood and on to the tarred lane at
Daveytown. Follow the lane to Criptor Cross. Turn right for WARD
BRIDGE/WOODTOWN. Cross the bridge and walk uphill to a cattle-grid.
Bear right onto a track UNSUITABLE FOR MOTOR VEHICLES. On reach-
ing the tarred lane go straight on. When the lane forks, bear right.
Sampford Spiney church has a handsome and locally characteristic
Perpendicular tower with tall pinnacles. Sparing use of the lawnmow-
er has allowed a carpet of wild flowers to thrive in the churchyard.

From the church, continue up the same lane. Do not take the footpath at Gees Farm but walk on for a further 100 m and take the waymarked footpath on the right just beyond Eastontown. Cut across the

4

The Dartmoor Inn, Merrivale, with the disused quarry behind it

rough grass ahead to a lane. Turn right, and immediately left up a track towards Pewtor Cottage. The cottage is surrounded by a high hedge; where the track turns sharply left at the end of the hedge, walk ahead on a NNE bearing following a well beaten path which soon becomes a stony track. Follow this round a small disused quarry, where many of the stones bear the marks of quarrymen's tools. Keep the wall on your right. Walk to the left of the Vixen Tor enclosure. This is one of several Dartmoor tors, such as Hound, Fox, Hare, Hart, Doe and Hen, which are named after animals. Vixen has the highest rock (28 m) of any Dartmoor tor, and is sometimes called 'the Sphinx' because of its shape.

Cross the brook and walk ahead, keeping the wall on your right.

On reaching the road turn right and follow the verge down past the Merrivale Quarry to the Dartmoor Inn, which has some interesting period photographs and china.

After refreshment, turn left out of the inn and follow the redundant section of old road to cross the River Walkham by the old turnpike road bridge. Retrace your steps to the car park.

The Dartmoor Inn

Tel: (01822) 890340. It was first recorded as an inn in 1841 when it was probably a coaching stop. It is made up of four or five 17th century cottages, though the dividing walls were removed thirty years ago to make the long bar with wooden ceilings we see today. In the 1950s the fireplace was attractively enlarged with granite from the nearby quarry. Merrivale, the last sizeable Dartmoor granite quarry, was closed in the 1990s but stands behind the Inn as a stark reminder of what was one of the moor's main industries.

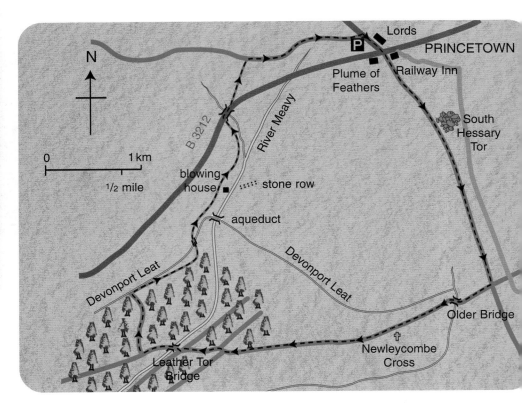

Walk 2 Princetown, South Hessary Tor and Black Tor

Distance: 12.5 km (7³/₄ miles)   Duration of walk: 4 hours
Character: A moorland and forest walk, mainly by defined paths. It is
less steep than most moorland routes, and has much of historical
interest as well as magnificent views.

Turn right out of Princetown car park (SX 589735). Walk past the
High Moorland Visitor Centre and take the bridleway between the
Railway Inn and the Plume of Feathers. It is a flat, broad path leading
to South Hessary Tor, which has a Victorian spike on its crown. This
is a boundary marker for Dartmoor Forest, one of only two left.

Walk on for another 1.6 km to a very clear junction of bridleways.
Turn right and head SW. Follow the track over the Devonport Leat at
Older Bridge and on by the old tin workings, the scars now covered by
grass and furze. Walk on to Newleycombe Cross, just to the left of the
track at SX 592703. This ancient cross, one of over a hundred on
Dartmoor, has been well restored. The original top portion has been
set in a new shaft, using the ancient socket stone.

Continue along the track, enjoying the views of Sheeps Tor and Burrator Reservoir. Enter woodland and turn right then left at a junction of tracks, PUBLIC BRIDLEPATH LEATHER TOR FARM. Continue descending to a 'crossroads': turn right for LEATHER TOR FARM AND COUNTY ROAD and start to ascend.

On the right after 150 m you will see a man-made cave, said to have been used by miners for storing potatoes: they stayed out here all the working week, far from their homes. 20 m beyond the cave, turn right over a stile for DEVONPORT LEAT. At the leat turn right, for STANLAKE FARM. Follow the path beside the leat and out of the woods by a stile.

Work began on the leat in 1793. It served the expanding community on the Devonport dockyard site until the construction of the Burrator Reservoir in 1898. Now diverted into Burrator, much of the leat remains as an integral part of local drainage. Trout abound.

Walk beside the leat and after 150 m cross by a clapper bridge. Continue upstream on the west bank to an aqueduct, which brings the leat down Raddick Hill, making a mini waterfall. Leave the leat here and follow the same NNE course along the path parallel to the infant River Meavy.

Follow the grassy path up, then bear right, nearing the river again, to Black Tor Falls and the ruins of a 17th century tin mill, marked 'Blowing House' on the OS map, because the waterwheel drove bellows which heated a furnace to smelt the ore. For centuries tin was the main source of Dartmoor's wealth. Although production peaked in Tudor times, the industry continued into the early 20th century. The

A local artist painted the double-sided pub sign of the Railway Inn, which shows locomotive 4410, the last to run on the Yelverton to Princetown railway

remains of trenches and mines are scattered all over the moor.

Continue up the west bank of the river. About 150 m beyond the blowing house ruins, on the opposite bank, you can see the Hart Tor double stone row, which is accessible in dry weather. It is 126 m long and ends at a cairn. A second cairn heads a shorter single row.

Continue more or less parallel to the river, but keep to the higher rougher ground along a rather indistinct path which runs between the tussocks of boggy ground and the slope of the hill on the left.

On meeting the Princetown Road, turn right across the bridge and after 50 m turn left into a rough path, aligning yourself a little to the right of the TV mast on North Hessary Tor. Reaching the trackbed of the old railway, turn right and follow the path back to Princetown, where in addition to the Railway Inn you will find other pubs and tea-rooms, including 'Lords'.

The Railway Inn

Tel: (01822) 890232. This pub recovered its old name in the 1990s, after some 40 years as the Devil's Elbow – probably from the bend on the road near Devil's Bridge. The Railway Inn was built in 1827 as the terminus of the horse-drawn Plymouth & Dartmoor Railway. Railway horses were stabled in what is now the Stable Bar, and the railway company used the inn buildings as a store.

By the 1880s profits had slumped. The line was taken over by the Great Western Railway and new track was laid. The last passenger service ran in 1956 and the rails were pulled up soon afterwards.

The stepping stones at Dartmeet, in the second part of the walk

Walk 3 Hexworthy and Dartmeet

Length: 10.5km (6 ¹/₂ miles)   Duration of walk: 3 ¹/₄ hours
Character: Field and moorland paths, bridleways and quiet lanes. The
views are magnificent. There is one steep ascent.
NB The second half of the walk has stepping stones and should not be
attempted after heavy rain. Parts of the route are wet underfoot.

The Forest Inn
Tel (01364) 631211 (to check parking availability)
www.theforestinn.co.uk

The Forest Inn enjoys a splendid situation in the midst of Dartmoor's grandest scenery. It was a favourite haunt of Dartmoor author William Crossing, who knew the old thatched building before it was ravaged by fire. The inn as we see it was completed in 1916 and bears the Prince of Wales' symbol – a plume of three feathers. Inside is a restaurant, easy chairs and an open fire, as well as Dartmoor landscape paintings by local artist David Young. Walkers are welcome.

Parking opposite the inn (SW 655726) is reserved for customers. Otherwise, park off-road on the lane leading uphill from the inn, or the lane branching right from this to Sherberton.

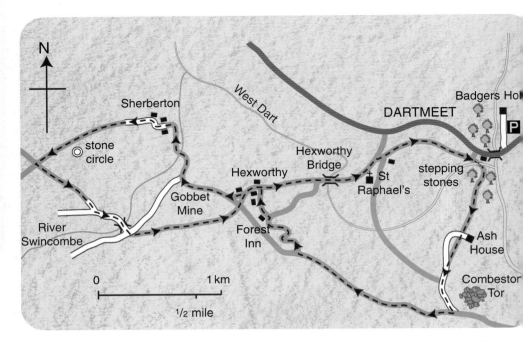

Take the lane in front of the inn with a No Through Road sign and follow it down to Hexworthy and then up. Immediately after Thimble Hall, turn left and walk uphill. Cross a tarmac access drive, then after 80m join a lane. Go through the metal gate signed SHERBERTON FARM and follow the lane down. On the left are the remains of the 19th century Gobbet Mine and a little further up the valley are the remains of older tin works.

Cross the bridge and walk up to Sherberton Farm. Take the PUBLIC BRIDLEPATH between the farm buildings; turn left in front of the saw-yard into an enclosed track. Continue through the next gate onto the open moor.

Follow the BRIDLEPATH sign ahead, keeping the wall and fence on your left. The stone circle in the far left corner of the field is worth seeing, though most of its stones have been lost to the nearby wall. Don't take the gate here, but walk uphill for a further 150m, keeping the wall on your left.

Leave the field by the gate at the PATH sign and follow the well-beaten path to a junction. Turn left for R. SWINCOMBE. After 600m cross the stile at the end of the field, and after 60m keep left, following the BRIDLEPATH to a footbridge. Cross over and walk ahead as signed.

Continue to the lane, cross over and retrace your steps to Thimble Hall.

Thimble Hall is on the left of this photograph

Either visit the inn now, or turn left opposite Thimble Hall on the PUBLIC FOOTPATH for the second loop of this walk. Go through the yard ahead and into the field. Follow the path sign and cross the stone stile at the far end of the field. Walk down to the tarred lane, cross Hexworthy Bridge and walk on to St Raphael's Church. Built in 1869 to serve this part of the huge Lydford parish, it was also used as a school. The children's desks are now pews – with inkwell holders still in evidence.

Take the next turning right, opposite Huccaby Farm. Do not take the gate in front of you but bear left uphill, to another gate with a warning about the stepping stones. Walk ahead following the yellow waymarks over the hill and down into an enclosed lane. The path leads into a field and down to a house. Follow the lane behind the house to visit Dartmeet, where Badgers Holt offers refreshments. The road bridge here is dated 1792 and belongs to the turnpike era: upstream a few metres is its predecessor, a clapper bridge which may be medieval in origin.

Retrace your steps to the path and turn left for COMBESTONE VIA STEPPING STONES. On the far side, take the well-beaten PUBLIC BRIDLE-PATH uphill through the trees and on through fields. At Ash House, walk ahead for HOLNE ROAD AT COMBESTONE TOR, then join a farm track. Continue on this track at the next junction.

On reaching the road, turn left to visit Combestone Tor, a fine granite pile showing characteristic horizontal weathering and a rock basin. Turn right onto the lane and follow it down over the bridge, then up again. Fork right (PRINCETOWN 6) when the road divides and walk down to the Forest Inn.

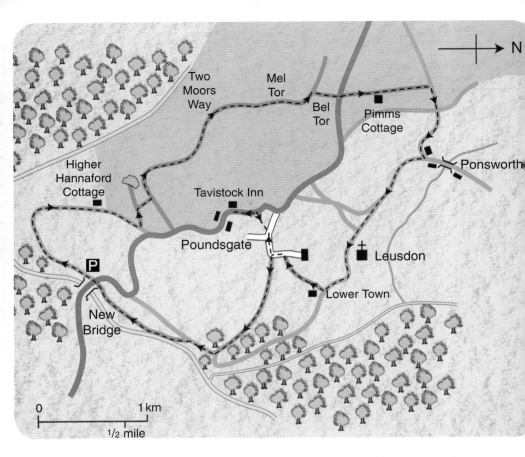

Walk 4 New Bridge, Dr Blackall's Drive and the Tavistock Inn

Distance: 11.3km (7 miles) Duration of walk: 4 hours
Character: A combination of beautiful moorland, woodland and
riverside walking along footpaths and quiet lanes. There are splendid
views of both the deeply eroded Dart valley and the surrounding tors.

Start from the car park (SX711709) by New Bridge – which is
medieval. Walk upriver along the minor lane from the back of the car
park. Stay with the lane as it diverges from the Dart. Continue uphill
past the Hannaford Farms.

About 500m after Higher Hannaford Cottage, a stony track joins
the road from the left: turn sharp left onto this – heading towards a
disused quarry – and then after 100m bear right uphill to meet a
broad track.

Turn left and follow this track (marked Two Moors Way and
Dartmoor Way on the OS map) for 2.5km. It is fairly level because it

12

was designed as a carriage drive in Victorian times by Dr Blackall for his invalid wife, to enable her to enjoy the wonderful vistas.

Beyond Mel Tor the track continues between stone walls. When it divides, turn 90° right and follow the stone wall up to the road at Bel Tor Corner. Cross over and continue ahead on the well-beaten path. Keep right down towards Primm Cottage, then follow the track to the left of the enclosure. At the end of the enclosure keep left and walk ahead to a tarred lane.

Turn right and walk past Looksgate Cross to Ponsworthy. Turn right for DARTMEET and walk on for 1 km. Bear left for LEUSDON CHURCH/LOWER TOWN. Pass the church and continue downhill for 350 m to a red post box on the right.

Turn right here and follow the track to a wooden gate with a yellow FOOTPATH sign. Walk on through fields as signed, keeping the hedge on your right. On reaching a lane, turn left. The next path junction has a tall fingerpost.

To visit the Tavistock Inn turn right up the lane. Keep right, into an avenue, then turn left through a spiky metal gate (PUBLIC FOOTPATH) beside a leat. Turn left onto the road, which can be busy, but the pub is only 250 m along it.

On leaving the pub, retrace your steps to the tall fingerpost. Walk

ahead through a metal gate, keeping the hedge on your left. On reaching Great Wood, fork left down the broad track (waymarked at the first stile) to a tarred lane. Turn right and take the next turning right for DARTMEET.

Follow the lane alongside the river, past the handsome lodge of Spitchwick Manor, until the lane diverts from the bank. Walk ahead across the meadow, keeping the river on your left. This is a fine bathing place in summer and ablaze with colour in the autumn, but most dramatic when the Dart is in spate. Walk on to New Bridge.

The Tavistock Inn

Tel: (01364) 631251. Medieval in origin, the Tavistock gets its name from being on the Ashburton to Tavistock Road. It is thought to have been a farmhouse before it became specialised as an inn, which is not uncommon – travellers in remote areas used to rely on roadside farms for their refreshment. Its ancient stone staircase is remarkable. Enjoy the beer garden with its flowers, or the comfortable bar with its log fires according to the season.

Trust you won't meet the Devil, who is said to have popped in one Sunday in 1638 on his way to destroy Widecombe Church by fire and thunder. The beer sizzled in his throat. He left scorch marks on the bar, and the seventeenth century equivalent of a bouncing cheque – his money turned to dry leaves as soon as he left!

Dartmoor in snow is magnificent – it's driving up there which is tricky!

Walk 5 Hay Tor, Hound Tor and the Rock Inn

Length: 11.5 km (7 1/4 miles) Duration of walk: 4 hours
Character: A walk combining great views with prehistoric and
industrial archaeology. Paths, quiet lanes and open moorland. Map
and compass essential.

The Rock Inn

Tel: (01364) 661305, www.rock-inn.co.uk. Built around 1826, along with the adjoining quarrymen's cottages, by quarry and tramway owner George Templer, the Rock was first a coaching inn, then a hotel. There are several period photographs in the bar – the Rock is instantly recognisable. There are also more recent photographs of Dartmoor life and people by local photographer Chris Chapman. Enjoy the colourful garden in summer, or in winter the log fire in the partly panelled bar, with its antiques and polished tables.Park at the main Hay Tor car park (SX765772).

Walk up the broad track to the summit of Haytor Rocks and enjoy the views, including Haldon, the Teign estuary, the South Hams and many Dartmoor tors. Walk due north along a narrow path through the heather to cross the path of the granite tramway. Take the broad track that leads on to Smallacombe Rocks.

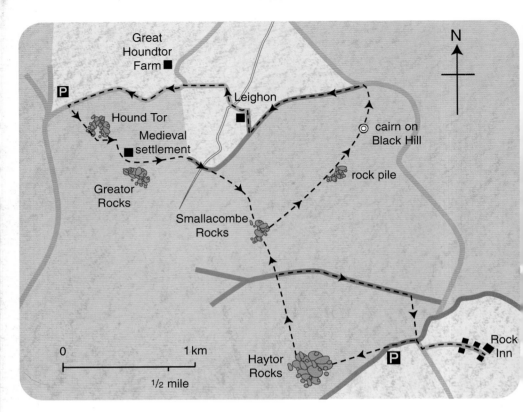

From Smallacombe Rocks, bear NE on the path through the heather leading to the rock pile on the brow of the hill. From the rock pile continue in the same direction to the cairn at the top of Black Hill, another wonderful viewpoint. Walk ahead downhill on a narrow path through the heather, aiming for the point where a track below you joins a tarmac lane.

Turn left along the track (not the lane) and after 900 m turn right, signed BY-WAY FOR LEIGHON. Walk past Leighon House, cross a stream, and bear left signed ROAD TO GREAT HOUNDTOR. At a road junction, keep left. The road soon begins to climb.

To explore Hound Tor, walk on over the cattle grid and then to the car park. Turn left and walk up to the summit. Legends of demon hounds associated with these fantastic rock piles fed the imagination of Sir Arthur Conan Doyle when he visited Dartmoor and added greatly to *The Hound of the Baskervilles*.

From the summit of Hound Tor walk SE down a broad grassy path to join the well-beaten path between Greator Rock and the fascinating remains of a medieval hamlet, one of 130 such settlements on

The Haytor Granite Tramway was Devon's first 'railway', opened in 1820 to transport quarried granite to a canal at Teigngrace, 12 km away – with its rails made from the granite instead of metal.

The full wagons descended by gravity, and the empties were hauled back by horses

Dartmoor and one of five to have been excavated. A farmstead, barns, pens, five longhouses and ancillary buildings are clearly outlined.

Follow the path to a gate on the left of Greator Rocks – PUBLIC BRI-DLEPATH LEIGHON VIA HAYTOR DOWN. The path descends steeply to a pretty clapper bridge. Walk on to a path junction. Do not turn left to LEIGHON, but continue uphill on an unsigned path. Follow this as it bears right near the top of the ridge and back to Smallacombe Rocks. This was a prehistoric settlement, and, bracken permitting, you should be able to find four impressive hut circles. (Prehistoric houses are generally round, medieval houses rectangular.)

Retrace your steps towards Haytor Rocks, but on reaching the tramway turn left along it and follow it eastward for 1 km. Then turn right down a path leading to the road near a red phone box.

Cross the road and head for HAYTOR VALE, over the cattle grid. Turn left for ROCK INN and walk down to it.

Retrace you steps uphill to the cattle grid and follow the road left (WIDECOMBE) to the car park.

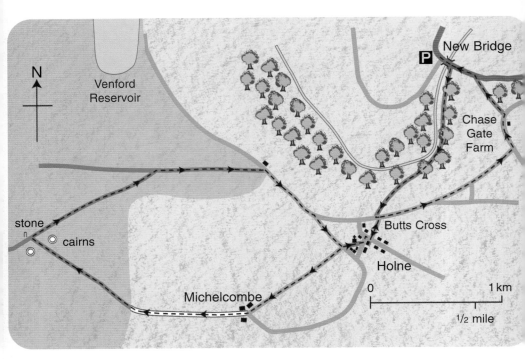

Walk 6 Holne and the Church House Inn

Distance: 10.5km (6 1/2 miles)   Duration of walk: 3 1/2 hours
Character: A figure of eight walk combining excellent moorland views
with a lovely riverside stretch and rural scenery. Both the Church
House Inn and the parish church in Holne are of considerable interest.
Compass and map desirable. At the time of writing the inn was closed
on Mondays, but it's worth checking, tel (01364) 631208.

Turn right out of the New Bridge car park (SX711709). Cross the
bridge (15th century) and turn right to enter HOLNE WOODS, following the MW (Two Moors Way) signed footpath. Broad and well-sur-
faced, this follows the river closely to a path division. Bear left and
uphill for HOLNE on a well beaten path, which leads through fields
and over stiles to a tarred lane.

Turn left and immediately right at Butts Cross for HOLNE VILLAGE
CENTRE. The Church House stands at the next junction, with the
church just beyond. It was probably built in the 13th century and, like
many Devon churches, was enlarged in the 15th. Both the superb
painted rood screen and the hourglass pulpit date from around 1500.

From the church porch, head diagonally right up the churchyard to
a kissing gate. Walk on, to a lane.

18

Take the lane ahead for MICHELCOMBE. On reaching the hamlet, take the NO THROUGH ROAD BRIDLEWAY ONLY. At the next path junction, walk ahead on BRIDLEPATH TO THE MOOR.

Follow the bridlepath steadily uphill to the moor gate. Continue ahead and uphill following the same (NW) course on a broad grass track. Cross a dry water channel (once the Wheal Emma leat) and continue until you reach two barrows and a boundary stone marked PUDC and RDH. Enjoy the tremendous vista, which includes Haytor Rocks, Rippon Tor and Hamel Down, as well as Buckland Beacon and the sea.

Now make a 90° turn to the right from the path by which you arrived and walk downhill (NE) on the beaten path. Venford Reservoir soon comes into view. On reaching the stony track bear right. Walk on down to a lane and bear right again.

Fork right at the next junction and walk down to the Michelcombe turn. Turn left a couple of metres beyond the junction and retrace your steps along the footpath to the church and the Church House Inn, then back to Butts Cross. Turn right there and keep left when the lane divides. At Stoney Post Cross, bear left for Ashburton. 100 m beyond Chase Gate Farm turn left onto the footpath for NEWBRIDGE.

On reaching the road, turn left and walk 250 m down to the car park. (Warning: this is a busy road by Dartmoor standards.)

The Church House Inn, Holne

Tel: (01364) 631208, www.Churchhouse-holne.co.uk. This was built in 1329 as a single-storey thatched house with granite walls. During the 15th century the porch and a second storey were added. The Kingsley Room has a beautifully carved screen. The room is named in honour of the Victorian writer Charles Kingsley, the author of *Westward Ho!* and *The Water Babies*, who was born at Holne in 1819, the son of the curate.

Holne's inn was earlier known as the Tavistock, like the nearby inn at Poundsgate (see page 14), but it became the Church House Inn around 1800. A photograph in the bar dated 1905 shows that the inn has not changed much in the last century.

As well as often providing accommodation for the priest, medieval church houses were commonly the venue for parish feasts, at which church ale was drunk. The proceeds went to the parish funds. Many later became church house inns – a relatively common name in Devon, where more than fifty still exist.

Walk 7   Scoriton, Huntingdon Cross and the Tradesman's Arms

Distance: 12.5 km (7³/₄ miles)   Duration of walk: 4 hours
Character: A walk with lovely views and full of archaeological interest,
including tin workings and a stone cross. Parts wet underfoot.
Map and compass essential. At the time of writing, the Tradesman's
Arms is closed Mondays and Tuesdays.

Park at the signed village hall car park (SX 704687) in Scoriton or at the Tradesman's Arms (phone first).

The Tradesman's Arms

Tel (01364) 631206, www.thepub@scoriton.net. 'Tradesman' originally referred to a craftsman (as in trades union) though it is more used today to mean a retailer. There is another Tradesman's Arms at Stokenham near Dartmouth, and one in Plymouth, as well as a Tradesman's at Bideford.

The Scoriton Inn is thought to be between two and three hundred years old and must have been a welcome sight for thirsty miners trekking back from the moor. Many would have used the Abbot's Way, by which we shall ourselves return.

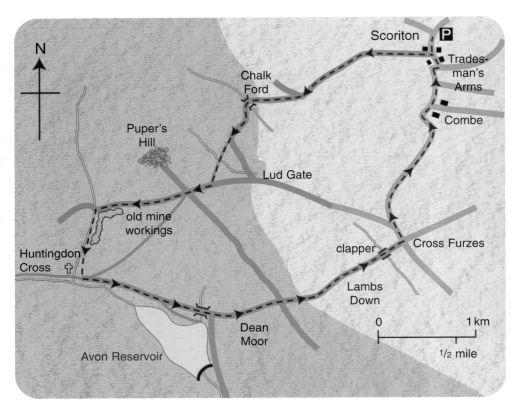

From the car park turn left, walk past the pub and turn right into a no through road. This soon becomes a stony track. Keep to the main track, uphill. At the next footpath sign ('MW' = Two Moors Way) keep left, CHALK FORD AND LUDGATE. Cross the brook by the footbridge at Chalk Ford and continue on the Two Moors Way LUDGATE FOR CROSS FURZES.

Follow the path uphill to the left through bracken and scrub. Splendid views open out. Keep going uphill. When the path bears off to the left, continue uphill in a SSW direction. When you strike the track which comes from Lud Gate, keep right, uphill and WSW. Do not be diverted by the various animal tracks.

Arriving at a junction of paths beneath the rock pile of Puper's Hill, walk ahead on the beaten track. This follows a westerly course, diverging from the Two Moors Way. Follow the track past old mine workings to the Western Wella Brook. Turn left and follow the eastern bank downstream, picking your way carefully to avoid wet ground. Tinners' waste, mostly covered in grass and heather, is strewn liberally around the banks.

The hamlet of Combe

Huntingdon Cross stands at the confluence of the infant River Avon and the Western Wella Brook (SX 665662), by a relatively recent but very well constructed dry stone wall. The cross was a boundary stone built *in situ* to mark the bounds of the Manor of Brent in 1557. Huntingdon Cross also marks the old ford across the Avon.

From Huntingdon Cross take the Abbot's Way, which linked the abbeys of Buckfast and Tavistock. Originally this was known as the Jobber's Path because wool jobbers, with their trains of packhorses laden with wool bales, used it to cross the moor.

Keep the Avon on your right. The Abbot's Way skirts the north bank of the Avon Reservoir, completed in 1957. When the water level drops during drought, the ruins of a medieval settlement and prehistoric hut circles are revealed.

Continue on the Abbot's Way (don't take the path to the right, nearer the reservoir). Ford a brook and walk over Dean Moor on a ENE bearing. Leave the open moor by a wooden gate, marked ABBOT'S WAY and keep to the waymarked path for CROSS FURZES as directed. Cross a stream at the bottom of Lamb's Down by a clapper bridge, marked 1703, 1737 and 1972 (when it was restored).

Walk up the track to a lane and turn left for COMBE/SCORITON. Fork right when the lane divides at Cross Furzes. Make the steep descent to Combe and the steep but shorter ascent towards Scoriton. At Whitey Cross, turn left for the Tradesman's Arms.

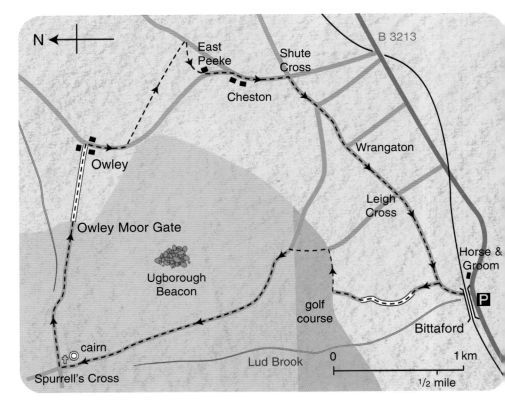

Walk 8   Bittaford, Spurrell's Cross and the Horse and Groom

Distance: 10.5 km (6 1/2 miles)   Duration of walk: 3 1/4 hours
Character: The initial long slow climb onto the moor is rewarded with
splendid views and a stretch of open moor. The return by field paths
and quiet lanes offers a pleasing contrast.

Park on the B3213 (the old A38), using the marked parking area
(SS 666570) by the railway viaduct and 50 m from the Horse and
Groom. Turn left up Wrangaton Road and under the viaduct. After a
short stiff climb, turn left into 'Hillside' where a sign in the hedge
reads PUBLIC FOOTPATH TO THE MOOR.

Walk on past houses and through a metal gate. Continue uphill, following the PATH signs. When the tarmac ends, continue on a grassy
path. Climb a stone stile onto the golf course and turn right as directed. Keep the wall to your right.

At the path junction opposite Leigh Lane turn left onto PERMITTED
BRIDLEPATH ACROSS GOLF COURSE (this is not marked on the OS map).
Walk between marker posts to a PUBLIC FOOTPATH fingerpost and

turn left. Two of the tors from Walk 9 lie ahead, Western Beacon to the left, and Butterdon Hill with its prominent ridge cairns (prehistoric tombs). Follow the beaten path as it circles around the hill, climbing gently, then settles to a NNW direction up the Lud Brook valley. The path passes beside a cairn and, 130 m beyond it, arrives at Spurrell's Cross. Spurrell's is a true guide and wayside cross, situated on the junction of an ancient track from Exeter to Plymouth and another (the Blackwood Path) from Erme Pound on the high moor to Wrangaton Cross – which we visit later in this walk.

Turn right at Spurrell's Cross and take the beaten path east and downhill to Owley Moor Gate, keeping to the right of the valley, then to the left of a horse-shoe shaped enclosure to arrive at Owley Moor Gate. Take the BRIDLEPATH OWLEY. Follow this enclosed track to a lane. Turn right.

Take the next footpath left TO A38 AT THE WOODPECKER. Follow this well beaten path down a track then through fields to a fingerpost beside a gate into a lane. Turn sharp right back up the field – at the time of writing the sign to EAST PEEKE was damaged, but the path was clear and leads to a stile. Cross the stile and keep the hedge on your right, then through a wooden gate to East Peeke with its attractive old-fashioned duck pond. The path passes right in front of the farmhouse and emerges onto a lane via a very low doorway. Turn left.

Walk on for WRANGATON at Cheston Cross. Bear right for WRANGATON at Shute Cross, and carry on at Marwoods Cross. Look out for the carved granite cross by the little green in Wrangaton, almost hidden in a hedge by a thatched cottage. Its very simple design may indicate an early (Saxon?) date. Walk on past Leigh Cross and the 'Moorhaven Village' to Bittaford and the Horse and Groom – tel (01752) 892358.

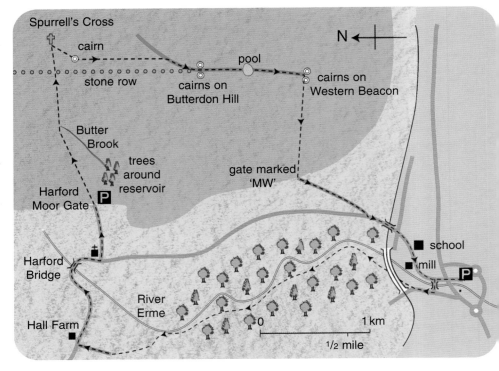

Walk 9 Ivybridge, Harford and Spurrell's Cross

Distance: 13.3km (8¼ miles)   Duration of walk: 4¼ hours
Character: A beautiful bankside path along the fast flowing Erme, then
a quiet lane to Harford and onto the open moor (compass and OS map
needed for safety). Ancient monuments and superb views.

Start from the town centre car parks in Ivybridge (SX 637561) where
the Leonards Road section has long-stay parking. Walk down to the
river (away from the ring-road) and turn right upriver along the path
and past a terrace. At the road junction, go forward into Harford Road
past a short-stay car park with a 1937 water turbine.

Turn left over the Erme by a small, high arched bridge. Turn right
into Station Road and walk on to Stowford Paper Mills. Take the path
by an information board, into IVYBRIDGE COMMUNITY WOODLAND.
Walk on under the eight-arched 1893 railway viaduct. The granite
piers for Brunel's original 1848 timber viaduct stand behind.

Follow the bankside path for the next 2.5km, over several stiles
until a PATH sign directs you away from the river. Walk uphill through
trees and over a pair of stiles to a path junction. Turn right, through a
wooden gate. Follow a series of PATH signs through the wood. Turn

right into the field as signed and walk across the next field to join a track, to the left of a dry stone wall; keep right, over a brook and through a gate.

On reaching the tarmac lane, turn right and walk on to Harford Church. This stands beside an old road from Plympton to South Brent which crossed the Erme (as we did) by the 16th century Harford Bridge. It then continued (as we shall) via Spurrell's Cross.

Leave the church by the south gate. Turn left and uphill past the School House to Harford Moor Gate. Continue in the same direction (ENE) over open ground. Cross the Butter Brook near the top of its little valley and head for a low mound on the skyline ahead, which looks like a barrow but isn't one. Just before you reach it you will cross a path beside the Butterdon Hill stone row – 2 km long, the second longest on the moor. Carry on ENE, crossing a disused railway track, and after about 300 m you should see Spurrell's Cross – not immediately visible but just over a brow of rising ground. (See page 25.)

From the cross, head SSW across rough grass and heather for 150 m. At the top of the slope you will find a cairn (at SX 658598). Now aim for the large cairns on Butterdon Hill to the south: you will pick up a broad grassy track leading to them, and to a triangulation pillar. From the pillar, take the track south towards Western Beacon, following a line of boundary stones and passing a pool.

From the cairns on the Western Beacon, turn west, aiming for the point at which two lines of trees intersect. Follow the broad grassy path down to a wooden gate marked MW (Two Moors Way). Take this track down to a tarmac lane. Turn left. Cross the railway bridge and walk ahead past a No Entry sign. Follow this road past the school and the paper mill back to the town centre, where you might try the Old Smithy (no food served though!) or the Exchange.

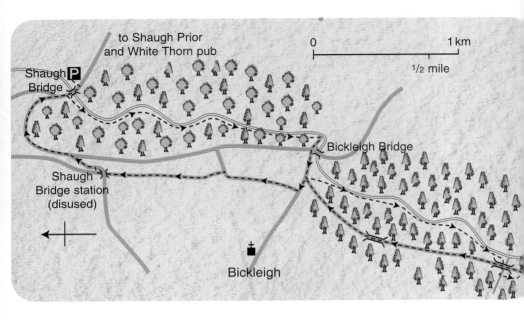

Walk 10   Shaugh Prior and the Plym Valley

Length: 9km (5¹/₂ miles)   Duration of walk: 2³/₄ hours
Character: We follow the beautiful river Plym through woods and
return via the Plym Valley Cycle Track, following the old Tavistock
railway line over three impressive viaducts.

Start at the popular car park near Shaugh Bridge. (There is another
car park the other side of the bridge if the main one is full.) Turn right
onto the lane and cross the bridge. Turn left along a signed footpath
downstream along the river bank for 2km. On reaching a footbridge,
do not cross but continue along the bank towards PLYM BRIDGE.

Just before Bickleigh Bridge, leave the riverside path at a NO ACCESS
sign and turn right. On reaching the lane, cross it and walk ahead
uphill for 250m. Turn left onto FOOTPATH TO PLYM BRIDGE. Take the
left path, not the cycle route. It descends steeply to rejoin the river.
Walk on for 1.2km, passing a fish ladder, a weir built to enable migra-
tory trout and salmon to swim upriver to spawn. On reaching a ford,
turn right under Riverford Viaduct, a fine piece of early 20th century
industrial architecture. Note the stone piers of the original 1859
Brunel viaduct beside it.

Cross the brook under the viaduct by a footbridge signed PLYM
BRIDGE. Don't follow the path on downriver. Climb the steep bank
ahead to the top of the viaduct. Turn left along the cycle track and

walk on. Bickleigh Viaduct gives a view of Bickleigh and Shaugh Prior.

On reaching a lane, turn left for GOODAMEAVY. 150 m ahead turn right, PLYM VALLEY CLEARBROOK. Follow the lane ahead to another PLYM VALLEY CLEARBROOK sign, then continue up the cycle track. Ham Green Bridge is popular with abseilers.

At Shaugh Bridge Station bear right onto the platform, then take the lane on the right downhill to the junction. Walk on a further 700m to Shaugh Bridge.

Shaugh Prior is a 1 km drive – or an unexciting walk – up the road. The White Thorn – tel: (01752) 839245 – is a 1930s replacement for an earlier inn, which is now 'White Thorn Cottage'. The cottage is over 200 years old and it is said that, like the Warren House Inn, it had a peat fire burning continuously for well over a century.

The village has a Church House with old chimneys and a staircase projection, and a Latin cross at a road junction, 100 m uphill from the church. The attractive cottages were built from 1830 onwards as housing for china clay workers. Parts of St Edward's church itself date back to the 11th century and it has excellent roof bosses and a painted ceilure. The 2.4 metre high late medieval font cover was discovered in a cattle shed in 1871 and sensitively restored by the prolific Exeter carver and sculptor Harry Hems (1842-1916).

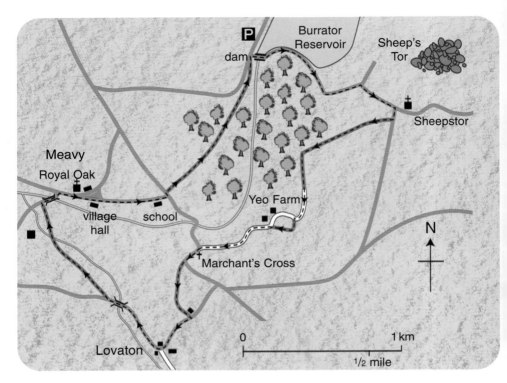

Walk 11 Sheepstor and Meavy

Distance: 7km (4½ miles)   Duration of walk: 2¼ hours
Character: A gentle moorland edge walk through fields and woods,
with fine views of Burrator Reservoir and surrounding moorland.
Two historic churches, three ancient crosses and a fine old inn add to
the interest.

Park on the roadside at the western end of Burrator Reservoir's dam
(SX551680). Walk along the dam and enjoy the view north to
Sharpitor. Finished with granite blocks in 1898 and a triumph of
Victorian engineering, the dam has now melded beautifully into the
landscape.

   Walk ahead to Sheepstor village. When the lane divides, keep right
towards the handsome 15th century granite church. It has many interesting features including a fine rood screen and carved bench ends.
There is a memorial to Sir James Brooke, the first White Rajah of
Sarawak, who is buried here with the other two White Rajahs. Their
story is told in some detail. Just south of the graveyard is a grassy area,
once used as a bullring. The iron ring to which the baited bull was
tethered was found here in a granite block.

Take the narrow lane opposite the ancient stone cross (restored in 1911) by the western entrance to the churchyard. Cross over the brook and 50 m ahead turn right, PUBLIC FOOTPATH MARCHANT'S CROSS. Cut diagonally across the first field, then follow the yellow waymarks, keeping near the wall on your right.

Cross a stone stile and enter an oak wood – full of bluebells in May. Climb down a ladder stile at the far end of the wood and turn right into an enclosed path. Follow the stiles and footpath signs around Yeo Farm (you are diverted to the left of the farm track). Bear left, signed PATH, along a tarmac track to Marchant' Cross.

At 2.4 m, Marchant's is the tallest of Dartmoor's old stone crosses and is 13th century or earlier. It served as a boundary marker between Meavy and Sheepstor parishes and probably marked and sanctified the Plympton Track between Tavistock Abbey and Plympton Priory.

Turn left and uphill for 150 m. Leave the road by a high stile, PUBLIC FOOTPATH LOVATON. Cut diagonally across fields (noting the upright stone in the second – another waymark on the ancient track?) to emerge on a lane at Cole Cottage. Turn right down the lane, past a telephone box. Cross the brook and after 80 m turn right at a stile, FOOTPATH TO MEAVY. Approaching the gate to Callisham Farm, turn right. Cross the brook by a small stone footbridge (it's about 20 m

upstream from the ford). Bear slightly left and join a track. Then cross over a stile into an enclosed path. On reaching the lane, turn right and right again for Meavy.

The Meavy Oak stands on the village green. The local tradition is that this oak dates to the time of King John (1199-1216) and connects it with the original Norman church, consecrated in 1122. However, one recent researcher suggested it probably dates from AD 1039. Next to the oak are St Peter's, a largely 15th century granite church, and the Royal Oak.

Walk eastward from the oak, past the village hall and on towards the school, where a replica of Drake's Drum stands in a glass case in the wall. Turn left for DOUSLAND and almost immediately right onto the PUBLIC FOOTPATH BURRATOR DAM. Follow the footpath by trees and through two wooden gates. When it divides, take the left path uphill through the trees to reach a leat marked PCWW 1917. Continue along the leat to the next fork. Bear left there, uphill to the dam.

The Royal Oak, Meavy

Tel: (01822) 852944. Like many Devon inns, this began as a church house. These precursors of the village hall hosted many social events, including 'church ales', when ale was specially brewed from donated malt; the proceeds of sale provided funds for the upkeep of the church.

Built of stone and cob, the Royal Oak was also used by monks travelling between their establishments at Buckfast, Plympton and Tavistock. Inside the right-hand bar is a cavernous log fire and a range of period and modern maps and photographs showing village life. A sketch of 1810 shows the inn as it was then, and a document of 1588/9 mentions it.